What You and The Devil Do to Stay Warm

Tyree Daye

What You and The Devil Do to Stay Warm

Tyree Daye

Blue Horse Press
P.O. Box 7000 - 760
Redondo Beach,
California   90277

Copyright 2015 by Tyree Daye ©

Cover photo: Tyree Daye

Editors: Jeffrey and Tobi Alfier

ISBN 978-0-6925-3219-5

Contents

Acknowledgements	iv
Fifth Street on Home	1
The Fall	3
Hydrangeas	4
The Devil's Funk	5
All God's Children Have Wings	6
Lake Johnson	7
How Twelve-Bar-Blues is Made	8
Sleep	9
The Devil Speaks	10
How Minimum Wage is Earned	11
Sulfur	12
Blues for Half Brothers	13
4th of July	14
How the Devil Keeps us Warm	15
Nassau Street	16
The Devil	17
Sing Nina	18
How I Love	19
How to Live with the Devil	20
ABOUT THE AUTHOR	22

Acknowledgments

Grateful to the following journals where the poems have appeared:

Jacar Press: "Blues for Half Brothers"

San Pedro River Review: "Sulfur"

Connotations Press: "Hydrangeas"

Thank you to my mother Joyce Anne Glover, DeLissa B. Smith, Dorianne Laux, Joseph Millar, Robert I. Greene and Jeffrey A. Langley

Babe, I don't care where you bury my body when I'm dead and gone.

~Robert Johnson

Fifth Street on Home

The only heater in the house was our Jesus
the Burger King below our church.
The value menu the bread, free water the blood.
The pope needed rent on the first
we were never on time. Liquor our holy oil.
No hallelujahs broke the quiet of the living room.
Robert Johnson our choir the one that could take us away.
If you cry about a nickel you'll die about a dime
and we were willing to. From Fifth Street
back home to Nazareth
you find a path and stick to it.
The same way you drive home in the rain
or walk through a mostly white grocery store.
It's all stars and street lamps when we disappear
into the blackest part of the street, avoiding cops.
The snow falls on the glazed-over-road
looks as if it's coming from hell.
We vowed if we made it through
what we started calling the devil's winter
with no friends junked-up on pills,
in love with the way they make you hum,
or attempting an old vaudeville suicide,

a show in blood, we would find God
or at least an agreeable shadow.
Jesus broke the heater one night
tired of our false worship.
The fireplace was too old for fires
and only created smoke. The sun reminds us
of what going to heaven could feel like. We took it in
let it burn off the night. We made
our normal rounds through the city.
First the convenience store where the owner
would give us bread and ham on credit.
When our toes were completely numb, God spoke
in his calm voice, the sink dripping overnight.
I rode the bus to the South Side and borrowed money
I couldn't pay back.

The Fall

When you buy dollar loaves of bread
you got a few days before the fungus sets in.
It's a sad thing praying over mold,
the devil sitting on the counter, the rat shit
pressed to his ass. He'll turn it into
a joke about the things dead men keep.
For now you just hear him laugh
every time you thank God for something.
I like to believe his little time in heaven did him good.
That he said a few *hail Marys* and *hallelujahs*
before the fall. And when he gives us dope
he's really saying something sweet, something
a mother would say before the juice takes hold.
That's how it goes, blues and buried,
bottles and Betty's. Until you come down
and you don't have quite enough
for beer across the street
and your credit is all run out.
So you go to your leftover butts,
picking out the wet ones.
Even the smoke you blow doesn't rise.

Hydrangeas

My gray umbilical cord was cut in July's heat.
I was washed and hidden
in the arms of a young woman
who years later hummed in a noiseless backyard,
her face lost behind sweat, dirt.
My job was to plant the purple hydrangeas beside the steps,
gain my grandmother's green-thumb badge.
You can't trust men she would say, "They would fuck
a glass of water if they could." Her legs would grow weak
before the summer ended,
the kidney cancer too far along.

The sun's heat burned every flower we had.

The Devil's Funk

He stands over my shoulder
his tail slapping my back. It's something
you could dance to. He's putting on a show,
he's on fire, taps my foot along.

There is no honor in finding firewood
after a rain, only gratefulness.
No horns will sound.
Your mother won't say she's proud of you.
She'll just tell you to come home.

All God's Children Have Wings

My great grandfather was a bootleg preacher
who sold liquor on Saturday evenings
while men with guitars sang about women
with long arms who walked out on them
before they could make it home
and say something sweet
to make her stay.
Then on Sunday mornings
before Miss Johnson caught the Holy Ghost
and the choir broke out into *As Long As I Got King Jesus*
he preached the gin out of you.

Jesus was the last word to leap
from his tongue, before he blew his
mighty head off. The name slurred in sermons,
grazed thighs, homemade wine and hallelujahs.

No one owns those blue jays beyond that oak
in that lone ash. God knows them
but they control their wings.

Lake Johnson

For Joe and Rob

We stringed fishing poles
trying to see the face of a Catfish.
I can only remember
the water now as a window
after one of those summer storms
children praise youth in.
You can't hear the city out here.
Can't smell the old Lincolns
leaking gas. Can't hear the transmission
slipping from second to third.
This could be the place
Jesus comes to sleep.

How Twelve-Bar-Blues is Made

Tab Benoit singing *Darkness*.
You're only there for the pain.
The rotting tooth you keep
smashing your tongue against.

You're only there for the face she makes
when she presses her chest to the sky and cries.
You're only there for the salt. The way
she stares at you when she's done.

Above, before God, the Seven Sisters compete
to be Big Mama Thornton singing
Gonna Leave You.
Matter must be like love to stars.

Sleep

for my Uncle Boo Boo

The walls have begun their questioning.
I keep thinking of how you died
in your sleep. It must been like
a saxophone and a trumpet
playing a B flat scale
as a woman sang like Gloria Lynne
and your body turned to jazz.

I decide to let the silence have her
the whiskey in her coffee mug
still bright brown. She ate her way
out of my heart and fell to the floor
in only the way she could.
My blood swirling around her mouth.
Her teeth spotted red and healthy.

How do hours become ungodly?
The darkness knows our contempt for it.

Only the drunks and poets stumble the streets stained black.

The Devil Speaks

I'm walking around your head
when I make you walk around your room sometimes,
and if you do find sleep
the darkness becomes touchable
and you're afraid of how well
you can see me there
just walking around your head
while I make you walk around your room.

How Minimum Wage is Earned

I started writing this poem on the bus.
I decide to get off at the Food Lion
where I once double bagged groceries
because most things will break before you get them home.
Where I was told my hair was too nappy or fussy for work.
That it offended their straightness.
Where old white women would ask
to run their fingers through it.
Or that I smelled funny how a customer complained
said maybe it was my dreads.
Or the manager before that one. Who waved
his small fat hand in the air and whipped it
and told me to get back on his register
If I would have said anything it would
have been a shotgun. Him and his whip
spread across the sign that said service
in the corner. So I went back to work.
7.58 an hour don't get you to heaven
but it gets you through the night
and walk home, and write a poem.

Sulfur

In his poor-man's rage, my father would bang
his hands against the thin walls, cursing God's name.
Hating how he had to let the water run
a little before the brown scales disappeared.

Among her new in-laws my mother
was not loved let alone liked
and her nervousness, that would later be diagnosed
and prayed for in the darkness of her bedroom,
did not help her with his protective sisters.

My cries must have made him pace the whole trailer
each scream a reminder of everything
he didn't have. Like the men my parents
watched on the late shows. The only time
she would see him smile was after
Dick Van Dyke tripped on the stool
during the credits when it collapsed.

It was the old pine in the front yard
blowing brown needles everywhere
that did it, that made him leave us
with the spring. His hat low,
walking against the dirt-throwing wind of his life.

Blues for Half Brothers

Let's pretend that when we were little
we lived in the same house and it had a basement
and the darkness it held
could take up an entire Saturday.

Let's pretend our father didn't love
coke-bottle-shape women so much,
let's know our mothers were more
than a sugary taste.

Let's never say half when we call
each other "brothers." Let's call
everything else what it is and
let's only tell our secrets to God.

4th of July

My mother said you got butter, egg and sugar.
The sky broke out into booms.
Or snacks, maybe chips,
you got chips. I once sold his mother my only ten bag
because she looked liked she needed it more than me.
Him and his sisters stole frozen fries
from the Food Lion I worked at.
I didn't say anything when I saw them
walking out the door.
Neither one of us looking up.

How the Devil Keeps us Warm

Nights when we consider the cold holy,
the devil comes in the front door
from a busy day in hell holding something
behind his back like those TV dads.
We fall like children at his tail wagging
on the floor. His red becomes pink,
our eyes big. We're sure it's something
to put us to sleep. He says
when whiskey burns going down
that's him. We never liked that, but
we drank it down anyways.

Outside the city celebrates with sirens.

Nassau Street

Driftwood floats on a glazed pond
the Croaker want nothing but flies and light.
Someone is yelling for a child, after the third call
the voice loses its weight and wanders off.
A man sits on his porch his eye closed
praying to anything that has ears or at least eyes
to see the plea in his face. Out back the earth
just birthed a squash. The dirt spins in a breeze
and celebrates knowing it's not just for the dying.

Victor's blood made a pond
in a pot hole on the street. His mother swims in it.

It's easy to lose cardinals among a group of Nine-Trey Bloods
but they're there quiet looking for hawks.

There's nothing shining they can trust.

The Devil

Drugs get involved most nights,
he flicks the lighter and watches
it bounce on my face, smiles
calls me his schoolboy.
He becomes quiet when
I begin to praise and ask Jesus for things.
Starts fixing the holes in the windows, collects
firewood from out back, howls.
When I'm done and there's nothing left
but ash and the feeling you get
after you say amen, he'll ask how I feel
before he gives his nightly sermon.
He doesn't really care, I know
but I tell him anyways because
it's just him and a few rats
who come into the living room to listen.

Sing Nina

We both grew up smelling the
ancient pine. You the daughter
of a preacher, me the son of
a woman. The lord's
words tied around your
talented wrist. Your jazz chords
made Medgar Evers
ghost dance in Mississippi mud.

Sing Nina sing.

How I Love

Tonight while slicing bread I wanted to run
the blade over my hand and fill
a bucket, but really I just wanted to cry.

The man that lives in my head is an
asshole who only thinks with his dick
and screams while I'm trying to sleep.

I want to kill him but he has my father's eyes
and I can't look him straight on.

So if I tried I might miss and cut her smile.

How to Live with the Devil

He would stay up all night, his hands cupped
over the red eye of the stove. Planning our
next adventure, watching the rats gather what they could
before morning. I would hear him say her name
because he knew I was listening and she caused
an uneasiness in me. Made me lose part of myself.
Everyone slept in coats, double socks and hats.

We called him the devil
when we were mad.
Friend when he poured gin
in our cups and told us about a party
we could crash, raid the fridge
and dance home unseen. My mother
said he would leave me in a box
by an unnamed pond if I lied to her. If I stared
into a flame too long I would see him
horns and all.

If we let the rats tell it
it was their house, we only
junked it up with poor people's
treasures. Broken this and thats
we could sell for loose cigs and dollar
burgers when the stomach had enough
of waiting.

When all else failed we got drunk
on cheap wine and laughed
until the tears that
didn't question our manhood
broke loose and jumped.

Sometimes we talk about those nights
in a whisper, as if anything too loud
would possess us and we would
be inside the kitchen cleaning rat shit
off the counter. Tonight I'm going to call him up.
See who has taken his eye, held his hand.

ABOUT THE AUTHOR

Tyree Daye is a student in the North Carolina State University MFA program. He's been published in *San Pedro River Review, Prairie Schooner, Jacar Press, Connotation Press*. He has a chapbook entitled <u>Sea Island Blues</u> (Backbone Press).

www.ingramcontent.com/pod-product-compliance
Lightning Source LLC
Chambersburg PA
CBHW031311060426
42444CB00033B/1271